Love, –
Bill Anne

ORIENT

ORIENT

Hero Dog Guide of the Appalachian Trail

Text by Tom McMahon
Illustrations by Erin Mauterer

WRS
PUBLISHING

A Division of WRS Group, Inc.
Waco, Texas

First published in the United States of America in 1995
by WRS Publishing, a division of WRS Group, Inc.,
701 N. New Road, Waco, Texas 76710.
Book design by Kenneth Turbeville and Linda Filgo
Jacket design by Joe James

Printed in Hong Kong

10 9 8 7 6 5 4 3 2 1

Library of Congress Cataloging-in-Publication Data

McMahon, Tom, 1951-
        Orient : hero dog guide of the Appalachian Trail / text by Tom
McMahon : illustrated by Erin Mauterer.
        p.   cm.
        ISBN 1-56796-006-5 : $14.95
        1. Orient (Dog)--Juvenile literature. 2. Guide dogs--Appalachian
Trail--Juvenile literature. 3. Irwin, Bill, 1940-   --Juvenile
literature. 4. Blind--Appalachian Trail--Biography--Juvenile literature.
5. Blind--Travel--Appalachian Trail--Juvenile literature. 6. Hiking--
Appalachian Trail--Juvenile literature. [1. Orient (Dog) 2. Guide dogs.
3. Irwin, Bill, 1940-   . 4. Blind. 5. Physically handicapped.
6. Appalachian Trail.] I. Mauterer, Erin, ill. II. Title.
HV1780.M36   1995
636.7'0886--dc20   94-43642
                                                        CIP
                                                        AC

THE APPALACHIAN TRAIL

CANADA

N

ME
VT
NH
NY
MA
CT
NJ
PA
MD
WV
VA
NC
TN
GA

BEFORE YOU BEGIN
READING THIS STORY

Ask your mom or dad

or another adult you trust

to take you on a short "blind walk."

Close your eyes and let the adult

lead you safely around your house.

By feeling what it is like

to be blind, you will better

understand the adventure that

Orient is about to lead you on.

Orient woke up Jenny with a big wet lick on her cheek. "Good morning, Orient," Jenny replied with a sleepy smile.

Jenny looked over and admired her handsome German shepherd dog. She had adopted Orient when he was a tiny puppy. She was training him to be a working dog, and she knew that Orient would have to go to a special school soon. Jenny had given Orient lots of love and training during the past year. He was big and strong now – and smart.

Jenny knew that Orient was very special, but she had no idea that someday, a long time from now, he would be famous.

One day, Orient and Jenny ran in from the mailbox with a letter. "This is what I've been waiting for," said Jenny, as she waved the envelope at her parents and her younger brother, Nick.

"Yea, it's a letter from the dog guide school," cheered Jenny. After reading the letter, she looked down at Orient. "You're a very lucky dog. You get to go to school next week."

"Dogs don't go to school," said Nick after hearing the news.

"Some dogs do," replied his mom. "Orient has been selected to be a dog guide for a blind person. It's one of the most important jobs any dog could ever have."

"What does 'blind' mean?" Nick asked. "Well," answered his mom, "some people have eyes that don't work, so they can't see. Orient will go to a special school where he will learn how to help blind people get around safely."

A few days later, Orient left for school. Jenny and her family were sad to see Orient leave, but they knew that he would be a great friend and guide for a blind person.

7

Orient was very shy when he arrived at his new school. There were ten dogs in his class. Slowly, each of his classmates walked up to him, one at a time, and greeted him with a friendly sniff.

The next day, Orient and his classmates met their teacher. As the other dogs looked on, she called for Orient to come to her. She carefully put a big strap over Orient's head and back and attached it under his tummy.

"This is called a harness," said the teacher. "And it has a handle that a blind person can hold onto as you guide him." She held on to the handle as Orient proudly led her around the room.

Orient and the other dogs worked hard every day. They learned how to
 – respond to commands
 – stop at curbs
 – and guide their teacher around obstacles.

9

The big day finally
arrived. Orient would get to
meet his new blind master.
Orient had many questions.
Would his new owner be nice?
Where would they live?

Orient and his teacher
walked into a room where a
man sat quietly. Orient could
see the man, but because the
man was blind, he couldn't
see Orient. But the man knew
that Orient was in the room.
He could hear the click-click
of a dog's toenails on the floor.

Suddenly, a big smile spread across the man's face as he clapped his hands and said, "Orient." Orient ran across the room, put both front paws on the man's lap, and gave him a friendly lick.

"My name is Bill," said the man. "Would you like to come and live with me?"

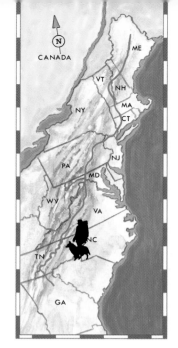

Orient went to live with Bill in North Carolina. He enjoyed helping Bill with errands in town. People and even other dogs stopped to watch Orient work.

Orient and Bill went for long walks every day. Orient didn't know it, but Bill was planning an adventure that would change their lives forever. Bill was planning a walk on one of the longest trails in the United States – the Appalachian Trail.

No blind person had ever done this before. There would be many dangers along the trail. Bill would need a lot of courage and his dog guide, Orient, to survive this long walk.

One morning, Bill whispered, "Orient, wake up. Do you want to go for a walk?" Orient barked his approval and ran to the front door.

A friend of Bill's drove them all the way to Georgia. They stopped next to a large, wooden sign. Orient jumped out of the car and led Bill to the sign. Bill could feel each of the letters on it. Bill grinned and said, "This is it! This is the beginning of the Appalachian Trail."

Orient noticed a white paint mark on a tree nearby. For the next 258 days, Orient would follow those white paint marks all the way to Maine – over 2,000 miles away.

"Forward," said Bill, and Orient began to lead him up the trail. They both carried packs on their backs. Bill carried his own food and water, his clothes, and the tent. Orient carried his favorite brush, his own food, and his bowl.

"Slow down, Orient," said Bill. "I've never seen you so excited."

Orient held his nose high in the air and enjoyed the fresh smells of the forest, but he always kept his eyes on the trail ahead.

Soon, Orient stopped in front of a large rock so Bill wouldn't fall. Bill walked over and felt the rock with his walking stick.

"Good boy, Orient," said Bill. "You saved me from tripping over that rock. But out here in the wilderness, there are lots of rocks like this. We can't stop at every one. Just keep going, Orient. I'll feel the next rock with my walking stick."

Orient was confused and afraid that Bill would fall over a rock. At school, his teacher had taught him to stop in front of anything that a blind person might fall over. Now, Bill was telling him something different.

Orient saw another large rock ahead, but this time he didn't warn Bill. Bill tripped over the rock and fell down.

"That's okay, Orient," groaned Bill as he got up. "I should have felt that rock with my walking stick. Let's go on."

Orient felt bad. He thought it was his fault that Bill had fallen.

Orient and Bill were
very tired by the end of
their first day on the trail.
Orient was so tired that he
barely touched his food. Bill
had fallen five more times,
and his knees were very
sore. He wondered if he and
Orient would be able to
walk all the way to Maine.

After a few days, Orient had learned how to lead Bill on the trail. Some days, when the trail was flat and the weather was good, they would walk twenty miles in one day. But on the other days, when the weather was bad or the trail was rocky, they could walk only three or four miles.

Orient guided Bill every step of the way.

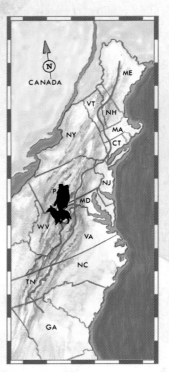

One evening, just as Bill and Orient were looking for a place to set up their tent, they heard a noise in the woods.

"GRRR, GRRR," growled Orient.

A much deeper and LOUDER growl came from the woods.

Then a bear appeared and came toward Orient and Bill. He could smell the food in their packs.

Standing between the bear and Bill, Orient growled even louder, "GRRR, GRRR." The bear stopped.

Just as Bill was trying to decide whether to throw down the food that he was carrying in the hope that the bear would leave him and Orient alone, the bear suddenly turned and ran down the trail. What a relief!

In Virginia, as Bill and Orient walked through the town of Damascus, they were asked to march in the Trail Days Parade with other hikers. Orient held his head high as he led Bill past the cheering crowd.

20

Orient and Bill were becoming famous. Every day, newspapers and the TV news reported that a blind man and his dog guide were trying to hike all the way to Maine. Millions of people across the country thought Bill and Orient were heroes. People everywhere were rooting for Bill and Orient to finish their long walk. But they still had many miles to go.

One morning Jenny woke up and was surprised to see Orient's picture in the paper. She missed Orient very much, but was happy that Orient was able to help Bill walk the trail.

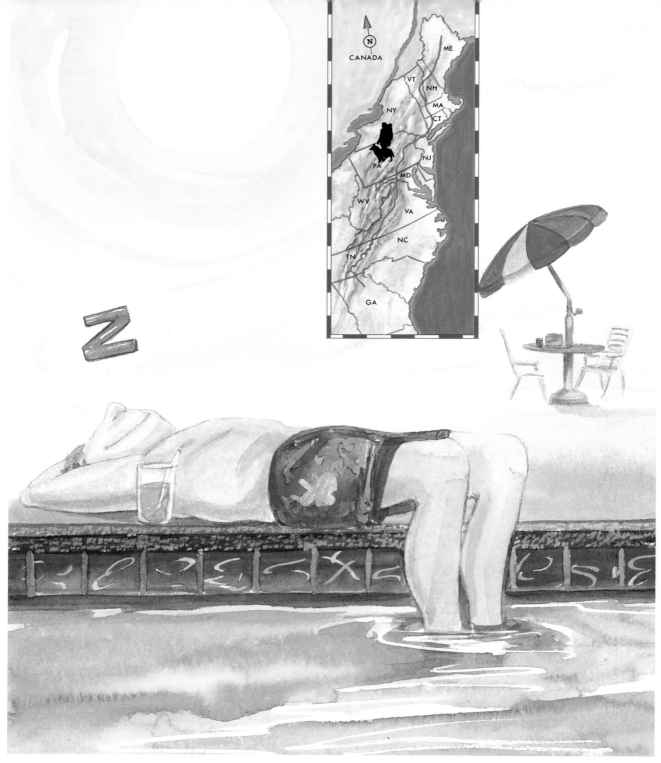

In Pennsylvania, with one-half of the trip completed, Bill and Orient decided to take a break from the trail. Orient was so tired that he slept at least eighteen hours a day for five days in a row. Bill spent most of his time soaking his tired feet in the swimming pool.

When they returned to the trail, Bill surprised Orient with four leather dog boots that he had made himself. The leather helped protect Orient's paws from the sharp rocks along the trail.

23

One night in Connecticut, Bill and Orient camped near some other hikers. Bill was sound asleep in his tent when he heard someone scream. "Help me!" yelled a camper. "A bear is trying to get me!"

Bill and the other campers raced out of their tents to help the man. They crept slowly toward the tent where the man was screaming for help. They could see the shadow of what looked like a big bear on the man's tent.

But it wasn't a bear at all – it was only Orient. His shadow on the tent had looked just like a bear. Everyone but the frightened man inside the tent laughed. The campers went back to bed, glad it hadn't been a real bear.

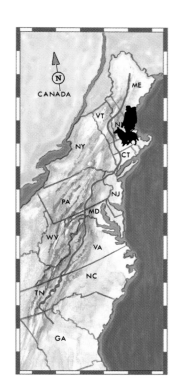

The weather got colder as Bill and Orient walked across New Hampshire and on toward Maine. The warm days of summer had been replaced by the cold and sometimes freezing weather of fall.

Bill wondered if he and Orient would be able to continue. But they kept walking north – climbing mountains, crossing icy rivers, and sometimes camping in pouring rain.

Whenever the trail went through a town or near a road, people would encourage them. "Hi, Bill!" they would yell from their cars. "Keep going… we're praying for you," shouted a woman from her kitchen window.

Children would always wave and cheer for Orient.

Bill and Orient were nearing the end of their journey. They had to walk only one more mile to reach the end of the trail. They were very tired. For eight months they had hiked up and down mountains, they had crossed many rivers and streams, and they had camped in every type of weather. They had also met hundreds of new friends along the way.

29

As Bill and Orient walked up to the last sign — the one marking the end of the trail — they were greeted by a big crowd of friends, relatives, and other hikers.

Many of these people had traveled hundreds of miles to celebrate this moment with Bill and Orient.

Bill dropped to his knees in front of the sign. The crowd was quiet. Bill silently thanked God for helping him make it to the end of the trail. And he thanked God for Orient – his guide and best friend.

The crowd cheered Bill and Orient.

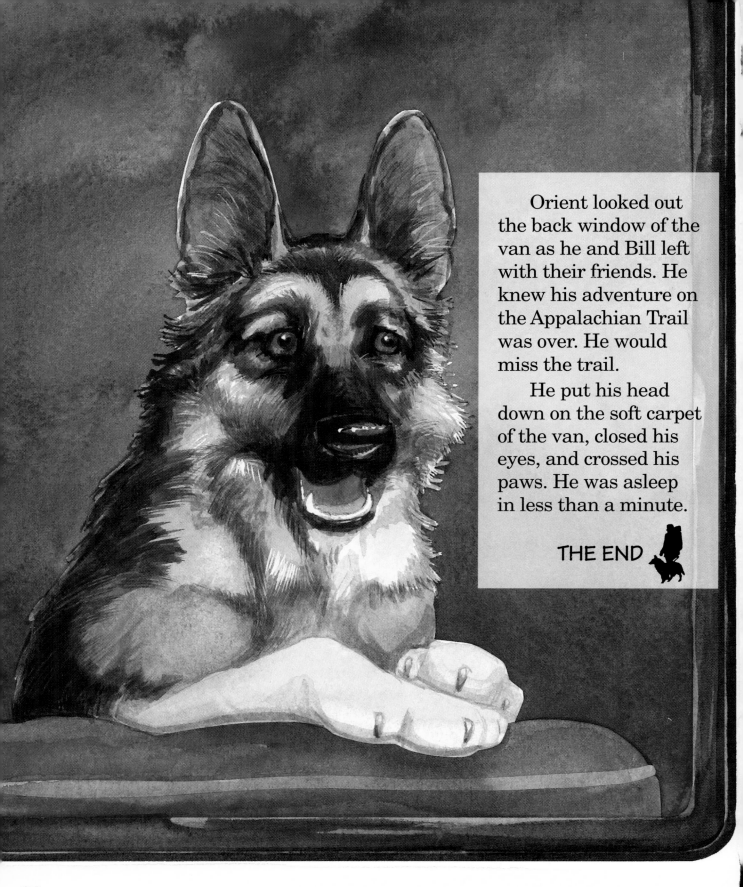

Orient looked out the back window of the van as he and Bill left with their friends. He knew his adventure on the Appalachian Trail was over. He would miss the trail.

He put his head down on the soft carpet of the van, closed his eyes, and crossed his paws. He was asleep in less than a minute.

THE END